Knights and Castles things to make and do

Leonie Pratt

Designed and illustrated by
Josephine Thompson, Kate Fearn and Katie Lovell

Edited by Fiona Watt

Steps illustrated by Molly Sage
Photographs by Howard Allman

Contents

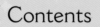

Jolly joust

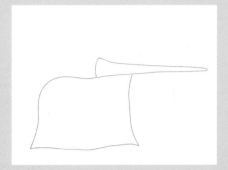

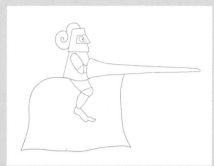

1. Draw a long thin shape for a lance on a piece of thin cardboard. Then, draw a shape for the horse's body below the lance, like this.

2. Add the knight's body, on top of the horse. Then, draw his helmet and face. Draw his arm holding the lance, then add a leg and a foot.

3. Draw wavy reins, then add the horse's head and tail. Fill everything in with felt-tip pens, then go over the pencil lines with a thin black pen.

You could draw lots of tents, then cut them out and glue them on the background.

Use the handles to slide the knights along the strip and make them charge into each other.

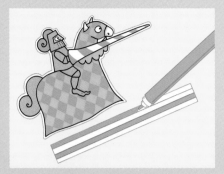

Glue the handle in the middle of the horse.

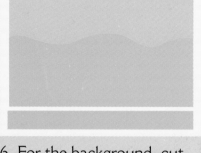

4. Cut around the horse and knight leaving a small border. Then, for a handle, cut a strip from thin cardboard and decorate it with felt-tip pens.

5. Fold over one end of the handle. Then, spread glue on the folded end and press it onto the back of the knight and horse.

6. For the background, cut a hill from green paper and glue it onto a big piece of blue cardboard. Cut a green strip as wide as the cardboard, too.

The handle on the horse and knight slides under the green strip.

7. Fold over both ends of the green strip and spread glue on them. Press the ends onto the hill, then slot the knight and horse under the strip.

Make another knight facing the other way for a joust.

Banquet painting

Press gently with your pencil as you draw.

1. Draw a straight line across a piece of paper for the table. Then, draw a shape like this above the line, for a prince's body.

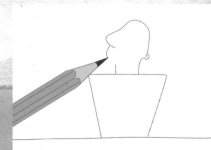

2. Add two lines for the neck. Draw a curve for the ear, then draw the top of the head and a big nose. Add a curve for the chin, too.

The crowns, goblets and fruit bowl were filled in using a gold pen.

3. Draw the eyes, mouth, hair and crown. Then, draw big curves for the arms, like this. Draw one hand resting on the table.

4. For a hand holding a goblet, draw a line for the back of the hand, then add four fingers. Draw the goblet, then add a thumb.

Draw one hand holding a glass.

5. Draw two curves for a princess's skirt. Add a square bodice, then draw circles for the shoulders. Then, draw the sleeves and hands.

You could add a hungry dog at the table, too.

The king was drawn in the same way as the prince, but using more rounded shapes.

6. Draw the princess's head and neck. Add a circle of hair on one side of her head, then draw the rest of her hair. Draw a face and crown, too.

7. Draw chairs around the figures and add food on the table. Then, fill in your picture using bright shades of watery paint.

8. When the paint is dry, use pencils to draw over the lines and add details on the clothes. Use a sharp pencil for the faces.

Silver sword

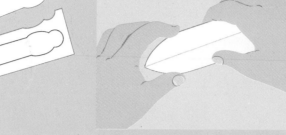

This will make
the sword 3-D.

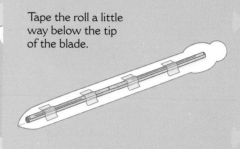

Tape the roll a little
way below the tip
of the blade.

1. Draw the blade and handle of a sword on a large piece of cardboard and cut it out. Draw around it, then cut out the second shape.

2. Pressing hard with a ballpoint pen, draw a line along the middle of each blade. Then, pinch the cardboard along the lines.

3. Cut a piece of newspaper as long as the blade. Roll the paper tightly and secure it with sticky tape. Then, tape it inside one of the blades.

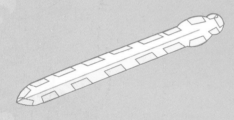

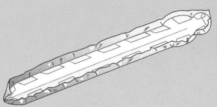

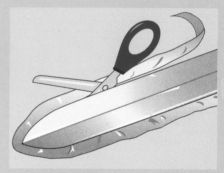

4. Lay the other shape on top of the roll so that the edges line up. Then, tape all the edges together with small pieces of sticky tape.

5. Cut a long piece of foil and glue it onto one side of the sword, shiny-side up. Fold over any overlapping edges and tape them.

6. Cut another long piece of foil. Glue the foil onto the other side of the sword, then cut off any foil that overlaps the edges.

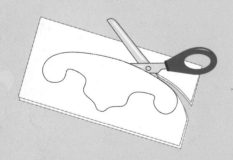

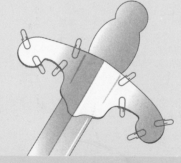

7. Fold a piece of thick paper in half. Draw a shape for the hand guard, then cut it out through both layers. Glue foil onto one side of each shape.

8. Glue the shapes around the sword, next to the handle. Use paper clips to hold the shapes in place until the glue has dried.

Start winding here.

Tuck the end in here.

9. Cut a long piece of string and tape one end of it onto the handle. Wind the string tightly around the handle, then tuck in the loose end.

The patterns on this handle were drawn on the foil by pressing hard with a blunt pencil.

Some swords were given names. King Arthur's sword, Excalibur is probably the most famous.

Fighting knights

Add sequins or stickers for a pair of spurs.

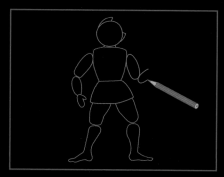

1. Draw a circle for a knight's head, then add a crest on top and a visor on one side. Draw a shape for the body, then add the arms and legs.

2. Use thick white paint to fill in the knight. Then, when the paint is dry, use a red chalk or a chalk pastel to draw a plume on the helmet.

Make one piece from each half a little bigger than the others.

3. Draw a circle on some foil to make joints for the elbows, shoulders and knees. Cut out the circle, then cut it in half. Cut each half into three parts.

4. Glue the bigger pieces on the knight's shoulders and the other pieces on his knees and elbows. Then, glue sequins on each joint and on the helmet.

5. Decorate the helmet and the bottom of the body using a silver pen. Then, draw curly patterns on the arms and legs using glitter glue.

You could use stickers from the middle of this book to decorate your knight.

6. Use sequins and shapes cut from shiny paper to decorate the knight's body. Then, cut out a sword and glue it onto one of his hands.

Draw circles with the glitter glue to get a chain mail effect, like on this knight.

Knights followed a 'code of chivalry'. This meant they had to behave well at all times – even when they were fighting.

3-D castle card

1. Cut a wide strip of thin cardboard and fold it in half. Bend the folded edge into the middle, then fold the other side on top.

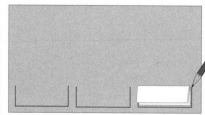

These shapes will be the three different parts of the castle.

2. Lay the folded strip on some paper. Draw along the bottom and the sides of it, to make three shapes along the bottom of the paper, like this.

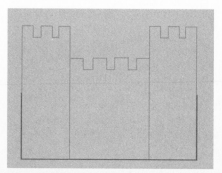

3. Inside one shape, draw two small towers with a gatehouse between them. Then, add battlements along the tops of the buildings.

The last tower needs to be the tallest.

4. Draw three taller towers on the second shape. On the last shape, draw some high battlements, with a very big tower in the middle.

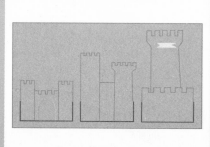

5. Cut out a door and a flag from different papers. Then, glue the door on the gatehouse and the flag near the top of the big tower.

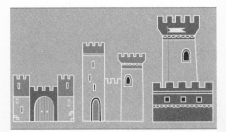

6. Fill in parts of the castle and add some windows using felt-tip pens. Outline everything with a silver pen, then add bricks and a flagpole.

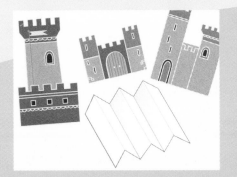

You could cut out paper roofs and glue them on in step 5.

7. Cut around the parts of the castle. Then, unfold the paper strip and crease all the folds so that the strip stands up in a zigzag, like this.

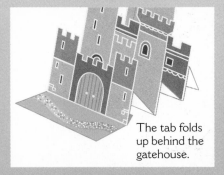

The tab folds up behind the gatehouse.

8. Glue the three parts of the castle onto the zigzag so that the big tower is at the back and the gatehouse is at the front.

9. Cut out a green paper rectangle that is as wide as the castle, for some grass. Then, cut a wavy river from shiny paper.

10. Glue the river onto the grass. Fold up one long edge of the paper to make a tab, then glue it onto the back of the gatehouse.

11

Dancing knights

The knight's arms and legs move so you can make him dance.

If you don't have any shiny cardboard, glue some foil onto thin cardboard instead.

1. Draw a knight's helmet on shiny cardboard, using a blunt pencil. Draw two eyes on white paper, then cut them out and glue them on.

Draw the arms and legs separately.

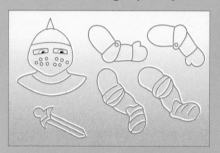

2. Add the bottom part of the helmet. Then, draw the arms, legs and a sword on the same piece of cardboard. Cut out all the shapes.

3. Cut a body and shield from bright paper. Glue the shield onto one arm and the sword onto the other arm. Then, glue the head onto the body.

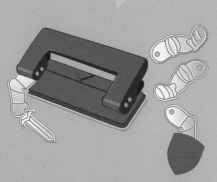

4. Use a hole puncher to make a hole in the top of each arm and leg. Take care not to punch through the edges of the cardboard.

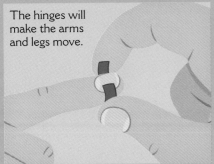

The hinges will make the arms and legs move.

You could use the ideas on these pages to make different kinds of knights.

5. Cut four thin strips of thick paper for the hinges. Lay your little finger in the middle of one strip, then fold up the strip on either side of it.

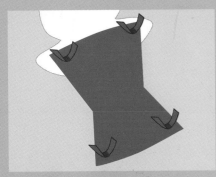

You may need to trim the ends a little.

6. Fold all the strips in the same way. Then, glue the middle of each hinge onto the back of the knight's body, one in each corner.

7. Push the ends of each hinge into the holes in the arms and legs. Then, fold the ends out, to secure the arms and legs.

13

Knight's helmet

1. For the jaw piece, cut a very long, wide strip of thin cardboard. The strip should go around your head, so that it covers your nose.

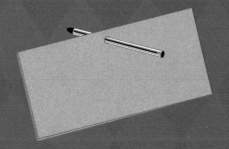

2. Fold the strip in half. Push a ballpoint pen through the cardboard, halfway along the strip, near the top. Make a hole in the other side, too.

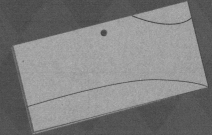

3. Draw two curves on the cardboard, like this. Then, keeping the strip folded, cut along the lines. Bend the strip around and tape the ends.

This silver helmet had textured foil glued onto the cardboard for the strips and visor.

The helmet below had decorations drawn on the visor and jaw piece before it was put together.

Although a visor protected a knight's eyes, it also stopped him from seeing very much!

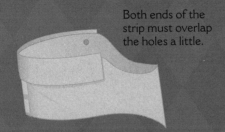

Both ends of the strip must overlap the holes a little.

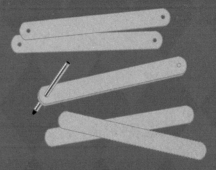

4. Cut a strip of cardboard. The strip must go around the back of the jaw piece, so the ends of the strip overlap the holes a little.

5. Cut the ends of the strip into curves. Draw a dot a little way in from each end, then push a ballpoint pen through each dot.

6. Draw around the shape five times on thin cardboard. Cut out the shapes, then make holes in the ends of each one using the first strip as a guide.

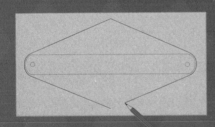

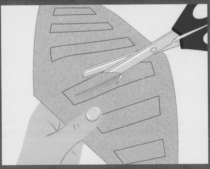

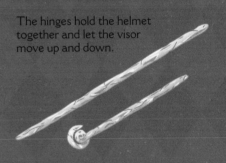

The hinges hold the helmet together and let the visor move up and down.

7. For the visor, draw around one of the strips. Add wide triangles above and below the shape. Then, cut it out and make holes in the ends.

8. Draw six rectangles with slanted ends on the visor. Pinch the middle of one and cut into it, then cut out the shape. Cut out all the shapes.

9. For the hinges, cut two strips of foil twice as long as your middle finger. Roll them into sticks, then twist one end of each into a thick spiral.

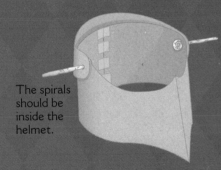

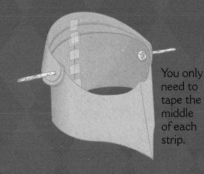

The spirals should be inside the helmet.

10. Push the sticks through the holes in the jaw piece. Thread a strip onto the sticks and move it until it overlaps the back of the jaw piece.

You only need to tape the middle of each strip.

11. Tape the strip onto the jaw piece. Add another strip that overlaps the first one and tape it in place. Add all the strips in the same way.

12. Add the visor last, but don't tape it onto a strip, so it can move up and down. Twist the loose ends of the foil sticks into tight spirals.

Dear Lord Laughsalot

Please come to my Jolly Joust
on Saturday at 1pm. I look forward
to knocking you off your horse.

Sir Fightsalot

PS Don't forget to bring your lance...
PPS ... or your horse!

Fleur-de-lis
is French for
lily flower. The
French royal
family used
it as their
badge.

You could use the stencil as a crest
on a letter or a gift tag, or print lots
of them to make wrapping paper.

Fleur-de-lis stencil

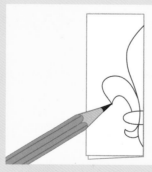

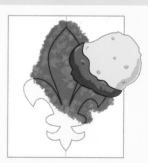

1. Fold a small piece of thick paper in half. Draw a long curving line against the fold. Then, add a small bump near the bottom.

2. Draw a small curly shape below the bump and a big one above it it. Then, keeping the paper folded, cut out the shape to make a stencil.

3. Open the stencil and lay it on some paper. Dip a sponge in thick paint, then dab paint over the stencil. Lift off the stencil and let the paint dry.

Pencil pennants

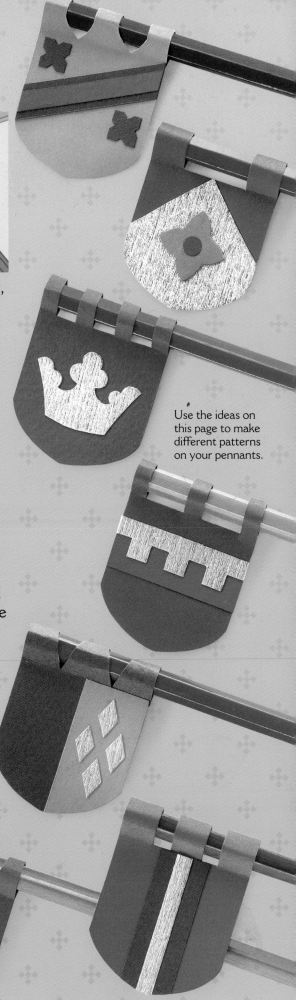

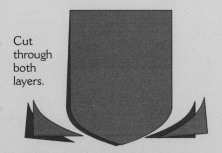

Cut through both layers.

1. Cut a small rectangle of bright paper and fold it in half. With the fold at the top, cut the bottom edge of the paper into a curve.

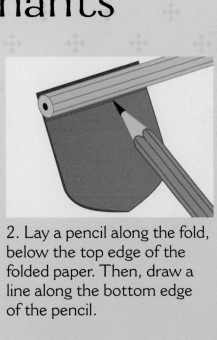

2. Lay a pencil along the fold, below the top edge of the folded paper. Then, draw a line along the bottom edge of the pencil.

Keep the paper folded as you cut out the shapes.

3. Draw two curved shapes between the line and the fold. Cut out the shapes, then unfold the paper so that you can still see the pencil line.

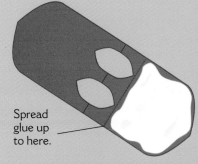

Spread glue up to here.

4. Spread glue on one side of the paper, up to the pencil line. Then, fold the other side of the paper on top of it and press it flat.

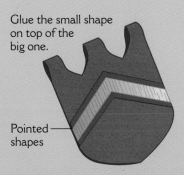

Glue the small shape on top of the big one.

Pointed shapes

5. Cut two pointed shapes from bright paper, making one bigger than the other. Glue them onto the pennant, with the points at the top.

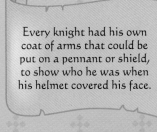

Every knight had his own coat of arms that could be put on a pennant or shield, to show who he was when his helmet covered his face.

Use the ideas on this page to make different patterns on your pennants.

Siege painting

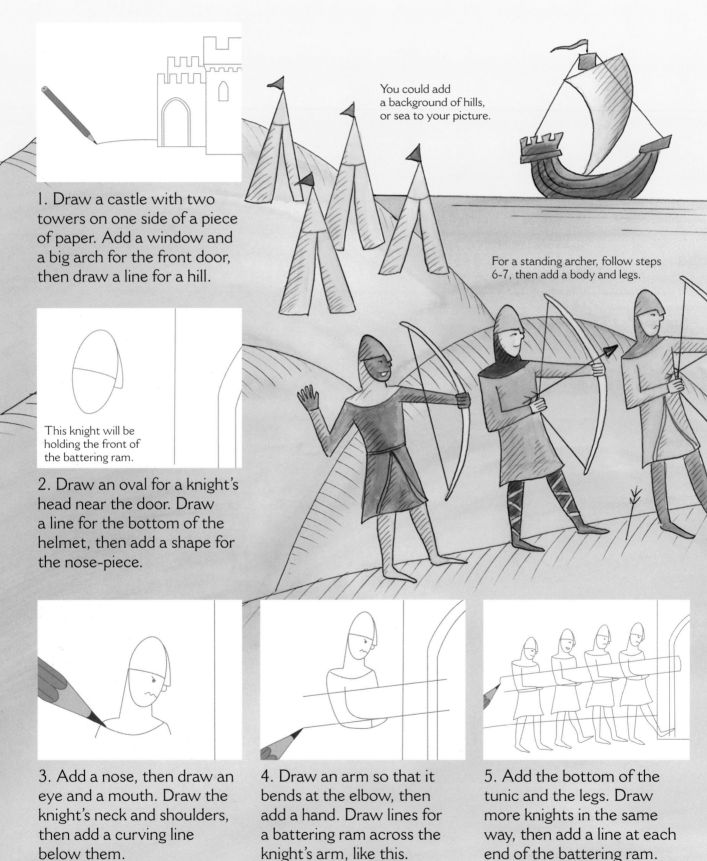

1. Draw a castle with two towers on one side of a piece of paper. Add a window and a big arch for the front door, then draw a line for a hill.

This knight will be holding the front of the battering ram.

2. Draw an oval for a knight's head near the door. Draw a line for the bottom of the helmet, then add a shape for the nose-piece.

You could add a background of hills, or sea to your picture.

For a standing archer, follow steps 6-7, then add a body and legs.

3. Add a nose, then draw an eye and a mouth. Draw the knight's neck and shoulders, then add a curving line below them.

4. Draw an arm so that it bends at the elbow, then add a hand. Draw lines for a battering ram across the knight's arm, like this.

5. Add the bottom of the tunic and the legs. Draw more knights in the same way, then add a line at each end of the battering ram.

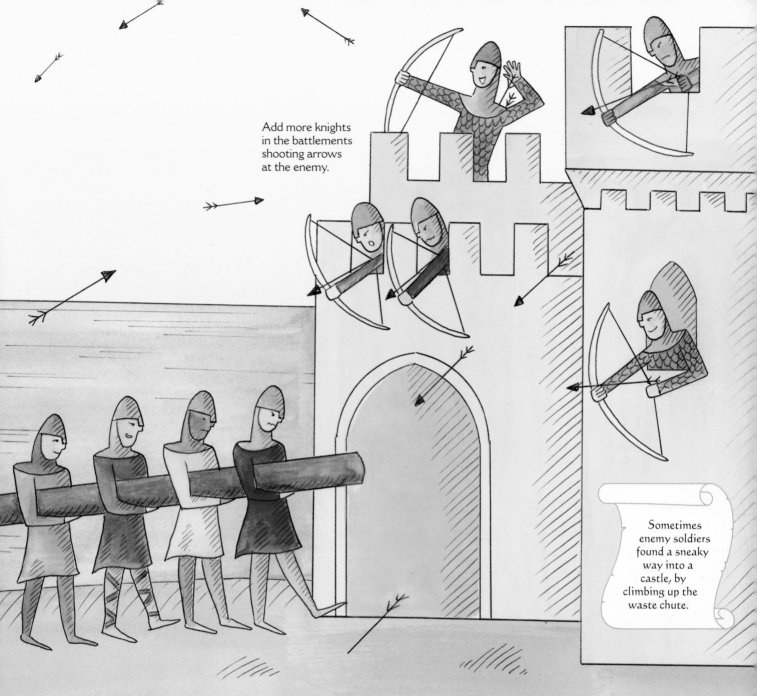

Add more knights in the battlements shooting arrows at the enemy.

Sometimes enemy soldiers found a sneaky way into a castle, by climbing up the waste chute.

6. For an archer, draw the head, neck and shoulders of a knight in the window. Then, add the arms, with one straight and one bent.

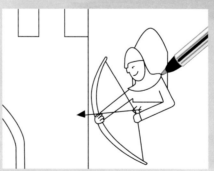

7. Draw round hands. Add a bow and arrow, then add fingers on the hand holding the bow. Draw over all the outlines with a ballpoint pen.

8. Add lines on all the knights and the castle, for shading. Then, fill in your picture using different shades of watery paint.

Castle tower

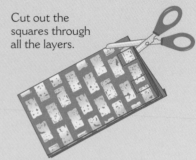

Dip the eraser in the paint again and again.

You will need the strip in step 11.

Cut out the squares through all the layers.

1. Cut a big rectangle from thin cardboard. Spread paint on an old plate. Dip an eraser in the paint and use it to print 'bricks' on the cardboard.

2. When the paint is dry, cut a strip from the rectangle and put it to the side. Then, fold over one edge of the big rectangle, to make a tab.

3. Keeping the tab folded, fold the rectangle in half, then in half again. Draw two squares on the top edge, then cut them out.

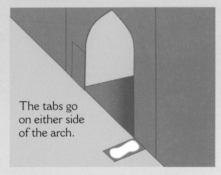

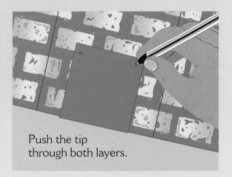

Draw the tabs at the bottom of the drawbridge.

The tabs go on either side of the arch.

Push the tip through both layers.

4. Unfold the castle. Cut an arch from the third section and lay it on a piece of paper. Draw a drawbridge around the arch and add two tabs.

5. Cut out the drawbridge. Fold up the tabs and spread glue on them. Then, press the tabs onto the back of the castle, like this.

6. Fold up the drawbridge. Then, push the tip of a ballpoint pen through the top corners of the drawbridge and the castle wall.

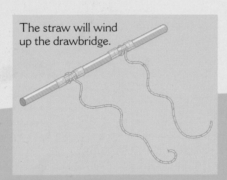

The holes should be at the same height.

The straw will wind up the drawbridge.

You may need to tie each knot twice.

7. Push a ballpoint pen all the way through the middle of the section to the left of the arch. Make a hole in the middle of the section on the right, too.

8. Cut two long pieces of thread, the same length. Tape one end of each piece onto a straw, leaving a space between them.

9. Push the threads through the holes in the front of the castle, then through the holes in the drawbridge. Tie knots in the ends.

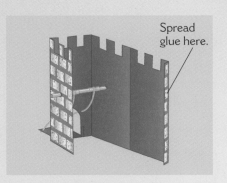

10. Bend the side walls around and push the straw through the side holes. Then, spread glue on the tab and bend the back around to make a square.

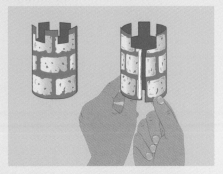

11. For turrets, cut the strip from step 2 in half. Cut squares into the top of each piece. Then, glue the ends of each piece together, like this.

12. Cut a slit on either side of the front two corners of the castle. Then, carefully slot the two round towers onto the castle.

Spread glue here.

You could cut flags and windows from paper and glue them onto the turrets.

Turn the straw to wind up the drawbridge.

Flying dragon

Start drawing on the right-hand side of your paper.

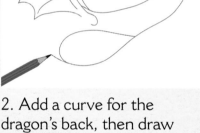

1. Draw a spiral for a dragon's nostril, then draw the top of the head. Add an oval eye, a horn and an ear. Then, draw the mouth with lots of teeth.

2. Add a curve for the dragon's back, then draw a big shape for the wing. Add another wing behind it. Then, draw the tummy.

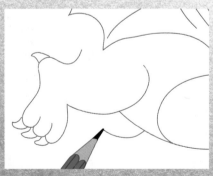

The knight will be here.

3. Draw curves for the back leg, and add a heel and three toes. Add claws on the toes and heel, then draw another leg behind the first one.

4. Draw a long, wavy tail. Draw a triangle on the tip of the tail, then draw lots of pointed scales along the dragon's back and neck.

5. Add two curving lines for the dragon's arm. Then, draw a thumb and three fingers. Draw another arm behind the first one.

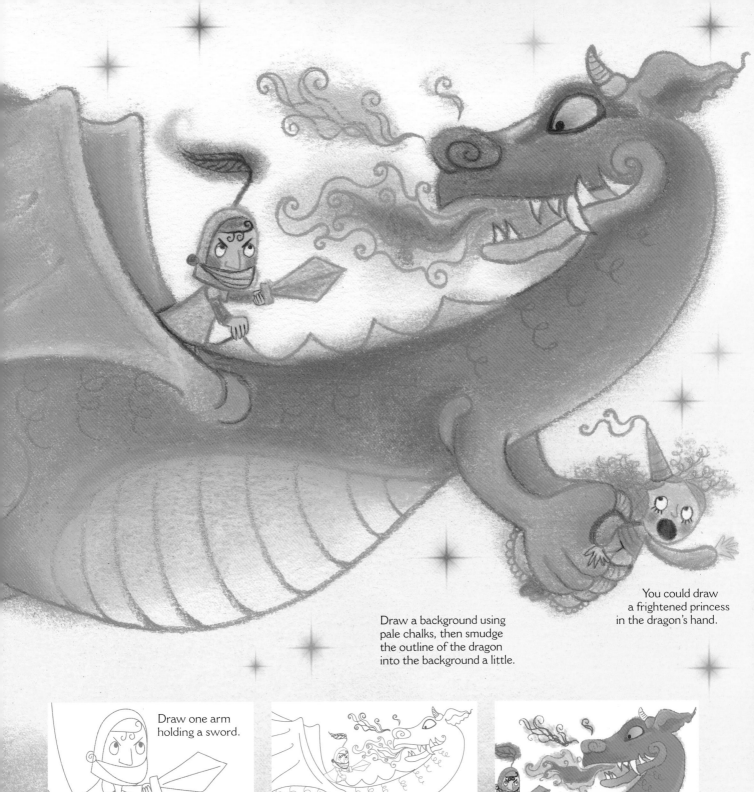

Draw a background using pale chalks, then smudge the outline of the dragon into the background a little.

You could draw a frightened princess in the dragon's hand.

Draw one arm holding a sword.

6. Draw the knight's body between the wings. Add a shape for the helmet, then draw the face. Draw the arms and add a sword, too.

7. Draw over the pencil lines using bright pencils. Then, add fire coming out of the dragon's mouth and smoke from the nostril.

8. Use bright shades of chalks or chalk pastels to fill in your drawing. Then, use your finger to smudge the chalks together a little.

23

Royal shield

1. Fold a large piece of thick red paper in half and draw half a shield against the fold. Then, keeping the paper folded, cut out the shield.

2. Unfold the shield and lay it on some thick cardboard. Draw around the shield, then cut it out. Put the cardboard shield to the side until step 4.

3. Cut the paper shield in half along the fold. Then, hold the two halves together again and cut them across the middle to make four pieces.

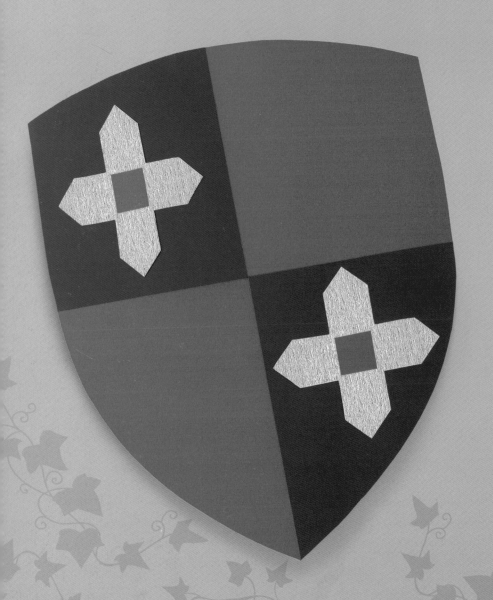

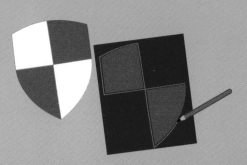

4. Glue two opposite pieces onto the cardboard shield. Draw around the other two pieces on blue paper and cut out the shapes.

You could add a red paper square in the middle of the shiny shapes.

5. Glue the blue pieces of paper onto the shield. Then, cut out two shapes from shiny paper and glue them on, too.

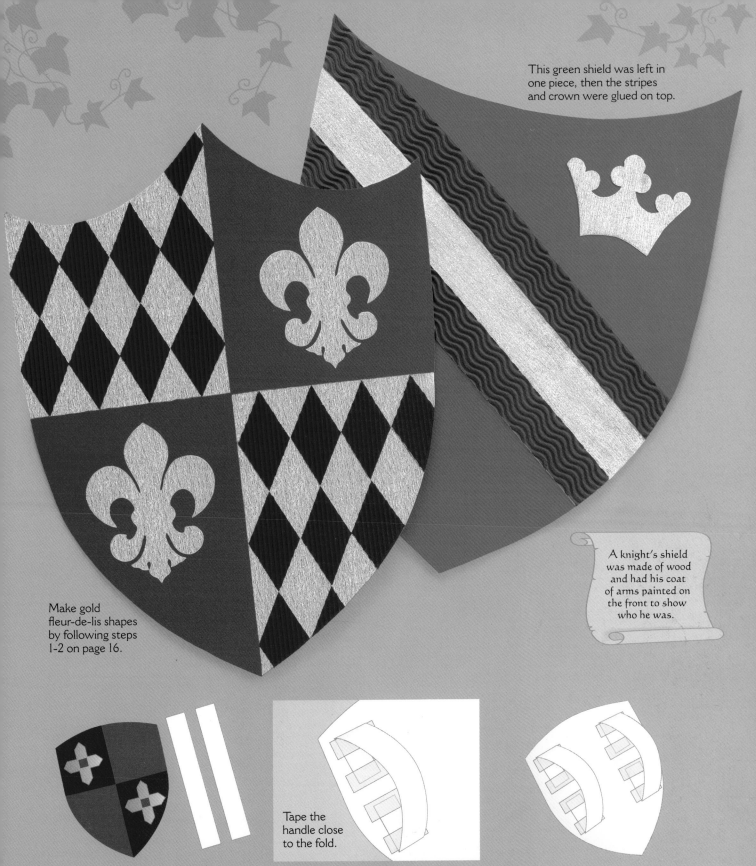

This green shield was left in one piece, then the stripes and crown were glued on top.

Make gold fleur-de-lis shapes by following steps 1-2 on page 16.

A knight's shield was made of wood and had his coat of arms painted on the front to show who he was.

Tape the handle close to the fold.

6. Cut two long strips from thin cardboard for the handles to go on the back of the shield. The strips should be as long as the shield.

7. Fold over both ends of one strip. Then, tape the ends onto one side of the back of the shield, so that the strip curves in the middle, like this.

8. Glue the other strip onto the other side of the shield in the same way. Then, gently bend the shield so that the front is slightly curved.

Castle characters

Use silver pen to draw netting on the princess's hair.

1. Cut a shape for a princess's skirt from bright paper and glue it onto some thin white cardboard. Cut out the body and arms and glue them on.

2. Draw the head, neck and two hands on a piece of white paper. Then, fill in the shapes with felt-tip pens and cut them out.

3. Glue the head on the top of the body and the hands onto the arms. Cut a shape for a tall hat and glue it on top of the head.

Use the ideas on these pages to make lots of different characters.

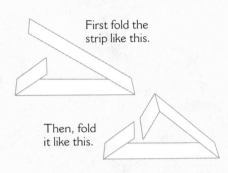

First fold the strip like this.

Then, fold it like this.

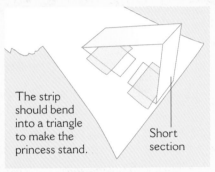

The strip should bend into a triangle to make the princess stand.

Short section

4. Cut different shapes from bright paper and glue them onto the dress and hat. Then, cut around the princess, leaving a small border.

5. Cut a strip from the thin cardboard and fold over one end. Keeping the end folded, fold the strip in half. Fold the other end inside the strip.

6. Open the strip. Tape the end of the short section onto the back of the princess, at the bottom. Tape the other end a little way above it.

For a page boy, knight, jester or king, cut out legs and feet instead of a skirt.

Cut out a crown for a queen or king.

27

Castle by night

1. Brush dark blue watery paint all over a piece of thick paper. While the paper is wet, brush stripes of purple paint on top. Leave the paint to dry.

The paints will bleed together.

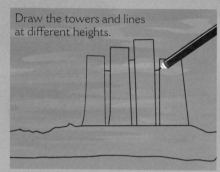

Draw the towers and lines at different heights.

2. Use a black pen to draw some land near the bottom of the paper. Then, draw four towers on one side. Add lines in between the towers.

3. Add turrets and pointed roofs on top of three of the towers, and battlements on top of the other one. Draw some windows, too.

4. Fill in the land and castle using thick black paint, taking care not to paint over the windows. Then, leave the paint to dry.

Draw flags on some of the spires.

5. Use a black felt-tip pen to draw wintry trees and grass on the land. Then, add details on the castle such as window frames and spires.

Draw lots of lines for the moon's reflection.

6. Draw a moon using white chalk. Add white shading along one side of each tower. Then, draw wavy lines on the land and in the water.

You could draw a knight galloping across the land.

These birds were
drawn with a
black felt-tip pen.

Stained glass window

You don't need this piece.

1. Fold a piece of black paper in half. Draw half an arch against the fold, for a window. Then, keeping the paper folded, cut out the arch.

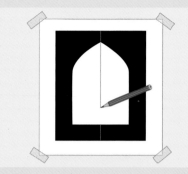

2. Tape a piece of white paper onto a work surface. Unfold the window and lay it on top, then draw a line down the middle of the arch.

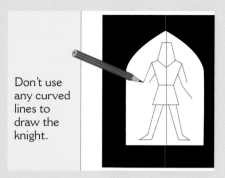

Don't use any curved lines to draw the knight.

3. Draw shapes for a knight's helmet and body at the top of the arch. Add the legs, then draw one bent arm and the top of the other arm.

4. Draw a sword below the bent arm and a shield below the other arm. Then, add lines coming out from the knight to the edge of the arch.

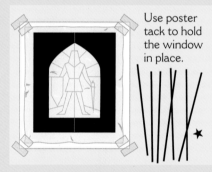

Use poster tack to hold the window in place.

5. Lay a big piece of plastic foodwrap over your drawing and lay the window on top. Then, cut lots of thin strips and a star from black paper.

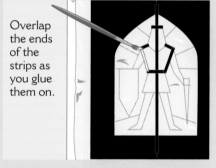

Overlap the ends of the strips as you glue them on.

6. Brush white glue down the middle of the arch and press a strip on top. Cut all the strips to fit over the lines in your drawing and glue them on.

Keep one blob white.

7. For the 'stained glass', squeeze several blobs of white glue onto an old plate. Then, mix different shades of food dye into each blob.

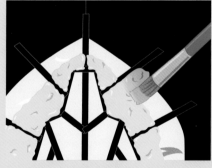

8. Brush a thick layer of yellow glue around the knight. Then, brush orange glue from the yellow out to the edge of the arch, like this.

Put the knight against a window so that light shines through it.

9. Use green glue at the bottom, then fill in the knight with other shades. Leave the glue to dry overnight, then peel off the foodwrap.

Fingerprint faces

You could draw a castle like this one with a different character inside each window.

This monk had lines drawn around his head, for hair.

For a guard, paint a helmet instead of hair.

Use your little finger to print the shoulders on a lady's dress, or bells on a jester's hat.

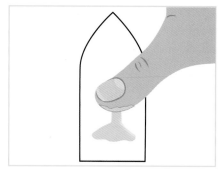

1. Draw an arched window. Then, mix some paint for the skin. Paint a lady's neck and shoulders, then use your thumb to print her head.

2. When the paint is dry, paint hair on top of the head. Then, use your little finger to print a circle of hair on either side of the head.

3. Paint a hat and the top of the dress. Add a pink dot for a mouth, too. When the paint is dry, use a thin black pen to draw a face and hair.

Photographic manipulation by Nick Wakeford
First published in 2006 by Usborne Publishing Ltd., 83-85 Saffron Hill, London, ECIN 8RT, England www.usborne.com
Copyright © 2006 Usborne Publishing Ltd. The name Usborne and the devices ♀ ⊕ are Trade Marks of Usborne Publishing Ltd.